James P. Lenfestey | *East Bluff*

James P. Lenfestey

East Bluff

MACKINAC POEMS OLD & NEW

Red Dragonfly Press

ISBN 978-1-945063-28-2 paper

Library of Congress Control Number: 2019945370

Designed and typeset at Red Dragonfly Press
   using Warnock Pro digital type

Printed in the United States of America
   on 30% recycled stock
   by BookMobile, a 100% wind-powered company

Published by Red Dragonfly Press
   P. O. Box 98
   Northfield, MN 55057

For more information and additional titles visit our website
   www.reddragonflypress.org

*It is not anything
you can take with you
into the next world,
this dawn.*

—Jim Moore

ACKNOWLEDGEMENTS

Gratitude to the Williams family for allowing me to marry their daughter Susan and for introducing me to Mackinac Island's East Bluff; to Susan for her love affair with the island that is passionate and organized; to my own family of loving memory for their many gifts of resources, inspiration, love of life and beauty and poetry; to Amelia Musser for asking me fifteen years ago to "do something" at the Grand Hotel after Shakespearean John McCabe passed away, and who did not flinch when I said I would offer "eight poets I love;" to poet and editor Thomas R. Smith, without whose gifted ear, unerring eye, and talent for manuscript organization I would publish no poems not to mention collections of poems; to the magazines and editors who have published a few of these poems—*Urthona, Voyageurs Region National Park Association Newsletter, River Images, Free Verse, Borealis, Cosmo Dogood's Urban Almanac, Poetry Notes, Nodin Poetry Anthology, Beneath the Lilac Canopy, Boomsite, Martin Lake Journal*—as most have been sequestered in my Macbook Air while I worked on other projects; and finally to Scott King of Red Dragonfly Press who again designed and printed my collection in an insanely short time, a giant gift to me and my island for the summer of 2019. Many of the poems in Part One, "Finding Your Tree, Your Bird," were published, a few in slightly different form, in a self-published chapbook, *Your Tree, Your Bird,* in six editions of 25, initially for the occasion of my reading at the Mackinac Island Public Library on June 29, 2001.

James P. Lenfestey
Minneapolis and Mackinac Island
Memorial Day, 2019

TABLE OF CONTENTS

INVOCATION

*"The etymologist finds the deadest word to have
once been a brilliant picture."*
– Emerson, *"The Poet"*

TROLLING

*"Alewife"— a species of herring invasive to the Great
Lakes, from "woman who keeps an alehouse," possibly
referencing the fish's fleshy belly.*

At dawn, fishing boats drop their silver
lines beneath the surface of the lake,
down where big-eyed salmon swallow alewives
and other slick allusives, some hiding a hook.

What other good words swim in the deep?
What syllables to hook the lip and tug the line?
To feed us as their eyes go pale, mouths gaping
at our feet, will they speak through me to you?

In the buoyant universe below,
fleshy barkeeps wipe rocky tables with
seaweed skirts, offering their generous bodies
to Coho and Chinook who belly up to swig.

There gleaming whitefish dance in swirls
and wave their gills, and solitary sturgeon loiter
at the dark end of the bar refusing to rise to any bait,
their etymology shadowy, obscure, armor-plated,
"perhaps from a lost pre-Indo-European tongue...."

We fishers at dawn are not ordinary men.
We embrace the food of solitude,
trolling back and forth, back and forth,
until a sound strikes our mouths with the taste of grace.

I

FINDING YOUR TREE, YOUR BIRD

I love all trees, but I am in love with pines.

– Aldo Leopold

YOUR TREE, YOUR BIRD

So where is it,
Your tree, your bird?
So when you sit,
cross-legged, palms out,
they come.
When you sleep,
they brush all around your bed.
And when you wake,
there's a familiar feather,
and a seed.

ZEN FOREST

Sun enters the Zen forest.
Still.
Cool.
No hurry.
Only questions:
Really, who are you?
Really, why is that
white pine?

THE WHITE PINE'S ANSWER

Distant caws.

And the unspeakable delicacy
of needles stirred by sunlight.

And broom fingers reach
toward the red squirrel's tender leap.

Above me, black embracing arms.
Below, five thighs
with a grip more fierce
than a hundred human lives.

Saying, lie down.
Here, rest.
Here everyone listens.

CEDARS SAY NOTHING

Even the catkins
of wild cherries
and the paddle fingers
of the locusts
speak in the wind.
Cedars say nothing.

When wind riffles their
wall of crowded hands,
fingertips of green amoebas
devour every sound,
leaving only umber duff.

Enter a cedar grove and
you'll hear
cries of gulls gone,
bell buoy clang gone,
ferry thrum, light
plane, all gone.

Breath gone,
pulse, heartbeat gone,
only soul sounds—
How long?
Why?

Then the elusive
wheeze of the warbler,
companion all along.

WHAT THE WHITE BIRCH KNOWS

A hundred feet above the lake
balances a bifurcated birch,
each arm bearing aloft the delicate crown.

Surely the trunk must split some day.
Just last year the fury of Lake Huron
mowed down nearby cedars
dared to grow too tall.

Yet it holds the edge—
twin torsos pitched against the wind.

And so our lives, mine and yours,
right in front of us,
impossible—

yet wearing a crown so green
all who pass bow low,
wishing it were theirs.

WHAT THE SPRUCE SHOWS

All over the island shore,
healthy babies.
Knee high and hand high,
head high and chest high,
fat and round,
bursting from stones.

Overhead, parents
scrape the sky
with ragged arms,
consumed by parasites.

On the ground, carcasses,
split in the middle,
collapsed into cedars,
sun-whitened bones akimbo.

Next to them, even more babies—
round, chubby,
green as grass.

SCREAMS OF THE BEECHES

All day I hear the screams
of the beeches,
collapsing,
defenseless
against
invading
blight.

Supple green to brittle bronze,
silver smooth skin
to scabrous scales,
resplendent crown to naked,
pleading arms,
rigid trunk to broken bones.

As the chestnut, blighted, gone.
Elm strangled, gone.
Ash slain by ash borer, gone.
Spruce toppled
by bud worm,
gone.

And the beeches,
screaming.

FOREST ROAD

"Hopkins invented 'dappled' for this."
— Zara Kublin

"Glory be to God for dappled things," sings Hopkins
here of asphalt stippled with gold and silver sunspots
touched down in tunneled hemlocks, cedars, spruce
on British Landing Road. Where soldiers and
natives once shot to kill, poets and children spin
delighted spokes downhill toward azure open water.
Past silent, sculpted cemetery stones,
cicada burr of light plane taking off,
hidden city compost raucous with gull talk,
golf link whack and horses' snort and whinny,
now two still miles of forest road dappled
with gold and silver for all to freely steal.

ABOVE THE BLUFF

From the wide porch, I watch
waxwings dive from birch branches
taking lake flies,
wood warblers bounce
along the stems of shimmering leaves,
yellow-eyed blackbirds strut
through dewed-diamond grass,
a ruby-throat's scarlet hover,
all under soaring shadows
of thieving ring-billed gulls.

Every tiny claw
and look and pass
makes my heart swell
as if Tolstoy wrote an epic
on my skin.
As if Chekhov set his
family's mad, disastrous laughter
beneath these trees.

WHAT THE CORMORANTS TELL

At dawn, a thread of cormorants
winds past the cedar cliff
toward nearby straits where
whitefish crowd in Indian nets.

Four long decades fishing birds
were gone from here, babies
crushed in their soft shells.

Back then, broken locals drank
sterno in abandoned cellars
and cedar woods were only
shingles waiting to be split.

Without cormorants, the lake
lay placid, sun-streaked, empty,
its sadness buried deep and cold
below this bursting heart of cedar cliffs.

CROW MORNINGS

Dawn caws, in threes, fours and sevens,
rasping hell sounds, yelling,
maybe a family group, the first fight
of the day. Or mobbing some intruder.

We are the intruders, two lazy sleepers
summer mornings in a bony cottage
with an eastward view a hundred miles
over water, and when we die, our children.

Black, accusing crows, lolling in gusts
at the bluff's edge, strutting the lawn,
calling disdainfully from spruce tops,
"Don't believe this place belongs to you!"

I worry in restless sleep about madness:
War, depression, children's tangles with roads
or spouses, a fouled planet, a failed life.
You worry out loud about the neighbor's beagle,
Great-horned owls, passing hawks and eagles.

You drive your woes away with a mad racket
and relentless aerial harassment.
Will you drive away our woes who
stupidly seek a bit of morning sleep?

Or will we, like you to us, adapt,
hear in your rattling caws
your firm insistence that no dawn
go unexperienced, not one sunrise
missed firing its gilded path to here.

Madness to miss even one, reason
enough to call to others
at the top of your lungs!

A BIRD I HAVE NEVER SEEN BEFORE

Right there, on the forest floor,
a bird I have never seen before.
I carried the pattern of its cheeks
for weeks, longing for its name.

And in my wonder, not one word
for this seeker of wild birds,
as if in an old uxorious room
where dreams may wake too soon

came flying from a birder's book
a solitary male. There! Look!
A naked, blathering, rough,
blind, wheezing, cough

of a man looking at the forest floor
at a bird he had never seen before–
a wandering, wobbling mound
of feathers starved for solitary sound.

FINDING A WOMAN'S SILVER HAIR
IN MY BIRD GUIDE

Who is this silent silver lover who,
when I'm away, thumbs down the
wonders of the warblers, the secrets
of the sparrows, that dark one
in and out of the low hedge
flicking its unimpressive tail?

I am the one who pauses conversations
for sudden birds, to watch and listen,
she resentful of interrupted human speech.

Yet in the quiet absence of my desire,
does she too wonder which dark tail
flicks under the fern, which singer
trembles her erotic ears?

THREE FLICKERS FEEDING

In raked dawn light, a flicker
father feeds a flicker child
leaving flicker shadows on the
flicker lawn, his tongue a light
while mother flicker laughs
and laughs and laughs.

As robin, puffing out her breast,
a deacon of this church,
drops in, as stirrings of
the morning breeze attest.

As overhead, the red eyes
of the vireo repeat, repeat, repeat
the lilt of lifting morning quilt.

I too now feed, an egg,
and praise the hunger
of the young, the
laughter of the old,
the light that wakes us up,
insists we sing.

EVERYTHING THIS MORNING IS GOLDEN

In the candelabra of the dead birch,
the warbler, roosting, is golden.
The ugly starlings are golden.
The patient doves,
the waxwings, as wicks, are golden.

Somewhere behind the cliff,
past the wall of thick cedar,
under the approaching quilt of storm,
the sun's lit match flares
over the sleeping belly of the lake
after the wild party last night
crowded with drunken stars.

The summer day has awakened,
and you and I with it—
like a mother giving birth
in a gush of glistening.
As the indigo bunting,
who is small, and loud,
and bold, and suddenly golden.

TEACHING POETRY TO OWLS

A fruitless task in early summer, Great
Horned babies screeching all night from cedar
branches for parents to feed them. Scree! Scree!

During the day, even, heedless young ones land
on the ground, unfurl their scary new wings
like huge eyes, even the dogs wary.

Not yet the frightening guttural questions
of adults — "Who? Who? Who are you?"
"Who full of why in the night?"
"Who trying to sleep but cannot" and so listen

to the babies' plaintive notes, "Scree, Scree,"
meaning "feed me, feed me," for which
ragged parents' work their magic wings,
feathers defeating all sound with softness
until the rabbit feels the needle claws
pierce its already broken neck, and the vole,
so adept at avoidance, suddenly becomes a pellet
of pressed fur and threaded bones, its life borrowed

by the silence of the night in which terrible
surprise lives and hunts and calls out
"Feed me, feed me," and answers with claws.

Poets too feed by listening and calling out,
mimicking the rusty screeches, mumbles,
moans and tremolo of older poets gone before.
Listening in the night, and calling out hunger
for syllables and the silences between,
"Feed me, feed me!" as talons of blood
and ink pierce the defenseless page.

II

PASSERS-BY

I myself write one or two indicative words for the future,
I but advance a moment only to wheel and hurry back in the darkness.

– Walt Whitman

PASSERS-BY
(August 26, 2013)

The sun, risen from the lake,
rakes over the bluff grass,
photons passing by one by one.

The Dunnigans, Marcia and Dan,
walk uphill into the wind,
arms around each other's waists.

Lily Levy passes, egret thin,
jeans flapping in the wind,
hair wild, wildly alone.

Betty rides uphill fast,
Bill walks slow,
both paint-spattered.

Water passes the Straits below,
deep as cities are tall,
rolling over every century or so,
the way cities roll over.

Rain clouds fall off to the east,
leaving behind
shiny roads, shimmering leaves.

The *Mesabi Miner*, low in the water,
"long as three football fields,"
shoulders aside islands.

My father rides by on a horse,
at full gallop, low in the saddle,
arms around the horse's neck.

Mother arrives as a bird, perfectly groomed,
fluttering off a waving tip of cedar,
her mother steady on the branch behind.

My wife bends in the garden, lifting
rain-heavy arms of blooming purple sage,
one by one, and other blossoms by name,
arranging beauty for all the passers-by.

NOT A BREATH OF WIND FOR THE SAILORS

Not a breath of wind,
as if the god of sailors spent,
exhausted in the thought of them,
so many sails to push with humid breath.

Let them languish then in pods, look down
like Narcissus at themselves, vanity
of their windy quest, as if not kings
but paupers in the steerage of their fate.

Remember, said the wind, I will not run
the wheel for you just you and you alone,
the biting bugs blown off your hides,

whether sails raise full for Troy or for the
"goat-like craggy guns of lofty Mackinaw,"
where friends await, woozy
with indifferent drinks, loud bands,

as quiet lovers of the land
pull their carts behind them,
filled with hay and grain,
clop clop they pull and go.

NOTE: *The phrase in quotation marks is Herman Melville,
from "The Lakeman's Tale" in* Moby Dick, *1851.*

DO YOU REGRET?

Do you regret, cedar tree,
waving your palms at dawn?
Do you, grasses, brushing seed heads
against the wind?
Do you, poison ivy, your name?
Or you, the lake, your murmuring?

You islands, floating without names,
swamped and useless, are you sad?
And you, old lighthouse, waving
your flag, restored, an icon,
useless but for memory?

You passengers on the ferry beating
into the sun? And away from the sun?
Your tears blow back like rain.

Trails through the woods, is your heart
broken at the direction offered and taken?
You hidden currents curled around islands,
a lazy S on the surface, we can see you!

You too bell buoy, stuck at anchor,
clanging and clanging,
are you sick of your warnings?

And you, shadows, deep at dawn as at dusk,
anchoring a shadow fence,
pointing through a forest trail to the lake,
the sea beyond and the sea beyond that,
is that not far enough?

Regrets in other languages, seen with
other eyes. But the clang and clang,
is that not the temple bell
dinging when the current strikes,
the deep gift given?

MOON CLOUDS

A shark with glowing mouth.
A man with dark glasses,
possibly a psychiatrist.
A devil's mask with fiery eyes.
A submarine surfacing through Arctic ice.

Oh cloud, oh moon, you play
so well together. We watch as you
turn Thomas Hart Benton skies
into our own vivid dreams.
Moon and cloud and me
and you, radiance
and revelation,

the predictable moon,
the surprise of cloud,
illumined darkness stealing
and surrendering,
leaving behind only
bright, astonished eyes.

"THE JAMES R. BARKER"

It's really not a ship at all.
More a billboard, a tipped-over
andiron, a protean water snake
swimming steadily, its thousand four foot
body unmoved by the wave break
splashing against its sides
as against a bedrock beach.

Hull made from itself,
plates thick as a wrist, heavy as the layers
of limestone a hundred fifty feet below
over which it glides
through the miracle of displacement
like a buoyant uprooted pine.

As if nothing these inland seas believed before
could make a difference in its life,
no storm make it shift and hunger
for the depths where stories lie,
no leviathan ever turn it back,
nor ever fear its dry dock fate
or wonder about itself, its belly
swelled with food for ingot furnaces,

as if the trail from mine to maw
made no difference to the tub of water
in which it freely soars, but for
a mild shudder on the shore.

EVEN SEAGULLS

Even seagulls, those pests,
flying at dusk,
carry golden bodies
to the evening roost,
to sit and chatter
in the lea of land.

Last night, under a double rainbow,
this thought:

Beauty is a trick of light
few birds care for.
Yet we grovel before the day's
resplendent openings
And closings as if a sexy
peacock's tail.

And if we dare, we gaze
at the mirrored sea,
too deep to reveal
a human face,
only the infernal bell buoy clang
from gravity's hidden sway.

Yet from that deep eukaryotic ooze
that gave us eyes and ears arose
a tiny birdlike, sun-illuminated thing—
A light? A song?
That, and only that, can save us.
Do you remember?

III

BLIND

What have you done with the garden that was entrusted to you?

– Antonio Machado,
translated by Robert Bly

BLIND:
SOLAR ECLIPSE, AUGUST 21, 2017

We look out on your once-in-a lifetime
darkening, leaving part of your light
to others for a day, sweeping sur-
prise across the oceans and vain
continents so careless with your light.

I took a hundred photographs,
stared through special lenses,
drank a toast to your rare absence,
swam in waters you refused
to evaporate this August day.

How blind we are, thinking this
visit, trapped by our cold moon,
reveals the truth, your golden
crown a glimpse of radiant heaven.

All other days you rise like a laborer,
boiling the horizon like the blacksmith's
forge you are, showering sparks
of treasure over upturned faces
with stone blind eyes,
44 watts per square meter
rarely gathered, rarely spent.
Except to lament that soon
enough we will want less of your
Godlike heat, more of the cold,
dark, silent, brooding moon.

AND SO THE DAWN HAS COME

I remember how the kayaks gathered
by the bell buoy, silent on the black glass
below the hundred cedar trees, cool
 limestone filtering the lake below.

They glowed as the fingers of the sun
reached for them, a friendly warning
or a hope, saying

This is the time this is the time this is the time
before song, before story, before worry,
before fear, before the soldiers of the day
who await on the other side of the trench

fix their bayonets, free at this moment
of murderous intent, free of grief
for the heat that lies before.

A mother stirs in her warm sheets.
She has forgotten all night her tormented child.
Then the tap of gold on the window pane,
a fluttering lid, the "Oh My God!"

ODE TO THE MICE IN MY KITCHEN

I will happily share my food with you,
and the grease under the stove,
and the drawer where you
leave your tiny bullets
among the potholders,
and the vents and ducts
in which you run.

But I will not share the stillness
of the dark before dawn
when I crave to be alone.

So when you race from beneath the stove,
crossing the rough kitchen boards like bison
thundering toward a cliff,
you startle this grumpy, slumped mountain
of glacier hair and ice blue eyes
lost in whirling mist.

So the trap must be baited again,
sprung back like an old watch.
But I will offer you a final benediction
for your scampering, intrusive lives.

I place two-year old aged white cheddar
from my home town creamery in Wisconsin
into the copper bowl, so when the spring
snaps on the back of your neck and pops
your black eyes out into twin
hatpin heads of astonishment and desire,
the last taste filling the twin caverns
between your whiskers
will be ambrosia.

ODE TO THE VOLE

Yes, you eating my wife's garden to a nub.
You, who have traveled across the desert space
of the walkway for a decade
like a harmless bullet,
we could set our clocks by you, if we had clocks,
so well trained are you by the attacks
from above, the owls, the hawks, the owls...

yet now you eat entire clumps of daisies,
bowls of lilies, and this rude anger surfaces,
to the point of traps baited with peanut butter.

And here is the first revelation. You love
peanut butter as I love peanut butter.

And so I hold your snout-snagged body
in my palm, and I see you for the first time
as vole, your pelt luminous and fine-haired,

and imagine trapping a thousand voles
and sewing them into a cloak
of one magical color
for her to wear to the ball
with ruby slippers and a yapping
candy-colored dog.

Of course the owls love you more,
traveling hundreds of miles to follow
your crowded irruptions, a wandering restaurant
of vole meat, but you still eat and eat and eat

your stealthy way into the heart of the garden
and simple-minded gardeners armed
only with ancient wooden traps, as you
feint with your nose and pelt
and breed and breed and breed.

THE SKY ONCE AGAIN TURNS LEADEN

What is wrong with me, to notice, even
with eyes deep in an immaculate book,
the persistent pollution of the world?

The sun ringed with it, a howling
calamity of taint, as if the very eye of God
were cindered, dimmed with cataracts,
welled with sorrow.

Today Heaven clouds with smoke
from fires searing five Western states
plus Yellow River soot and ash
clotting the plastic Pacific
(that once meant "Peace"),
drifting over miles of mountains
onto my horizon, blinkered
and red-rimmed with cell towers.

Like the black ant
foraging near my foot,
a soldier in the war to feed
a relentless queen demanding
the scraps of the failures of the living.

Have we descended from Mt. Olympus
only to follow scented chemical trails,
sparks of intelligence dulled as old copper,
colorless as a dry riverbed hunched
against drought, west wind bearing
the crimson feathers of a hundred monks
once high as gods on the Tibetan plateau,
self-immolated in their protest and despair,
saffron ash settled like spores
on the pupils of our eyes?

I melt further into the softness of my easy chair
filled with the down bodies of the dead,
and watch idly as the foraging ant
approaches the suppurating skin
of a damaged toe redolent with decay,
to which the taint from these ordinary exhalations
adds only another unwelcome chemical element.

SEPTEMBER GLARE

The sun on the sea is hard on the eyes
an hour past dawn the first of September.
Erupting below, brutal and boiling, swath
of molten mercury rolling up the shore,
the spectral fence failing its advance,
nor the forest nor the bluff's limestone edge,
light obliterating all in holy fire.

This is no angle of repose, this ravage,
but eyes forced down and in,
where the fear lies, where the lies live.

As the new god, pure fire, blackens northern forests,
Rainbow Lodge, sand banks, deer, black bear,
all blackened, all cooked, perhaps an osprey
escaped over boiling Superior waves.

Listen to the jay mock, undeterred,
mock, mock, at work today.
What will be *your* shouted cry?
What was it *you* wanted to say?

In the dark forest behind the wall,
a second mocking laugh, god
flicker, goose-necked woodpecker,
drives my head into the page,
mealy hunger for the food of words.

The way Hardy hungered for words
of light, not glare but flame,
a burn, a storm of morning,
searing white hot coal, a furnace
from which one dare not turn one's eye.

As I boy I visited with my father
the furnaces of J. R. Roebling's mill,

owned by Bethlehem Steel by then,
when Trenton was not a mockery
but the roaring heart of average dreams,
though not Thoreau's.

There new suns were made,
red hot and white hot,
from buckets hung overhead
drooling fire white as sunlight
into geometric blocks hammered
and squeezed into thumb-thick
wire spun red hot into cables
for the bridges of the world.

Past and future connected—
Brooklyn to Manhattan,
Golden Gate, Straits of Mackinac,
cable arcs a spider would admire,
framed above a tangled deck
of cars and trucks, and so...

here we are, or here I am,
point on a compass:
Not westward glow, southern swelter,
northern lights, but eastern burn
of blinding silver
boiled in a molten lake.

September glare drives me
from my comfortable chair
back to an attempt to see
what is lit inside of me.

O silver hammer,
O god of fire,
Bless me, turn me
not away!

AFTER THE STORM

Suddenly a light so bright
I can no longer read,
squinting like an Inuit hunter
far out on pack ice.

So I pull out my harpoon,
a Papermate Flair,
and mark my tracks
following clouds of slate
eastward over the lake.

Eyes slit, nostrils flared,
ears tremble for any sharp sound.
Weathered hands poise over
the breathing hole, then tread

on until the wild enthusiasms
of the birds return, and the
first monarchs of the season
claim title to the garden,
and every wet blossom
glisters and is gold.

IV

WHAT IS WIND, WHAT IS WATER?

To see a World in a grain of sand,
And Heaven in a Wild Flower...

– William Blake

YOU GET TO THE POINT WHEN YOU KNOW

You get to the point when you know
the difference between the tremble of
a leaf by wind,
and the tremble of a leaf by bird,
both hidden, both with another mind.

You get to the point when you know
that this dream is real, that one a
phantasm, one a chasm of despair,
the other a well of contentment.

You get to the point when you know
there is not enough money nor time
nor distance in this world to salve discontent,
nor enough discontent to undo
the inventions of wind, of water.

So much known, yet you still wake wondering,
like Magellan billowing forth round
the curve of unknown Earth,
from harrowing glacier passage
through a hundred blistering dawns:
What is wind, what is water?

LYING ALONE ON HURON'S STONY SHORE

Tiny little fairy feet, tiny
little fairy feet, tiny little
fairy feet tread under the
western wind.

Dancing cats prance up the shore,
dancing paws up the shore,
dainty paws dance up the shore,
under the western wind.

Shore stones tumble up
and down, clink and
clatter up and down,
under the western wind.

Thoughts flutter through my hair,
the thin few clouds,
The wide blank blue,
washed by the western wind.

Shadows of gulls, voices far,
arms of cedar wave and cheer.
Who says these are not for me,
under the western wind.

This shore, this sea, this feather
floating in transparency,
we float away on the waving world,
under the western wind.

What of the stones I do not know?
The stones I throw are swallowed whole.
I follow through that open door,
under the western wind.

TO THE ENGINEERS OF THE MACKINAC BRIDGE

Your graceful arcs nearly convince us
humans are worthy of this place—
a pail of fresh water sloshing back and forth
between the green poles of Heaven.

In the commerce of our lives, we look down
on waves, a range of mountains moving
at the drag of wind, a mobile fleet of
Rocky Mountains tumbling into glacier crests
filled with a thousand diamonds.

Unacknowledged Apollos of the professions,
engineers make mockery of water and time,
an achievement worthy to hang in a
New York City museum, an "installation"
in a galley between shores,
"enduring, sublime, ingenious, elegant,
practical and true," "one that
opens up new worlds," all raves.

As each wave slips below the bridge,
mangy and furious, clawing your smooth sides,
mermaids sing each to each, though
we do not hear them, too far below
the hum of tires on airy grids.

Only when we pause, distant and still,
will we hear the engineer's elegant strings
strummed by wind and sky,
mermaids clamoring below.

THE BUDDHA MOON

All is well as the sun plays taps.
The thieves have left the temple
to forage among their kind.
The dogs of war snarl and bark
at the old thin and spindly moon
a quarter turned away from chaos.

Here, when we cease to strive,
the moon rises round as Buddha's
belly, full of the fat of calm,
juiced by the bell buoy's chant
held firm in gravity's long sway.

The Buddha Moon,
so bright the wind
and the waves sing your praise.
And we humans, humbled
for the nonce, assume the open-
handed stance that nothing more
is needed for this day
than lowered lids,
and hands that pray.

MORNING FOG

Its blunt nose works its way
under the carpet of sunrise,
consuming dawn light,
leaving for those awake
rattling crow calls,
bell buoy clang,
foghorn moan,
gulls' complaints.

Or was it hands,
entwined in fingers of mist,
that tilted searching eyes
toward the sad dove's
five sigh song?

I tell you this: I saw close
on the window glass
a needle-legged spider
rework her lace.
Tell me:
Do you too hear her bobbins spinning?
Are you too dancing to her gypsy castanets?

THE SUN AT 70
(dawn, 7 September 2014)

The sun rises gently
from the lake and paints
its golden footprint to your feet.
You feel it is for you, is yours,
the way no photograph
can capture, though you click
and click and click from every angle
as the blossoms in the garden
gild one by one with golden light.

Soon enough a butterfly, the king,
will stretch impossible wings
filled with the liquid of your light,
just as my arms raise themselves
right now pulsing with your praise.

Let the day come, let the departure
schedule scroll, for the royal blue
has spread again across the dome of sky.

Let the birds raise their colorful throats,
the butterflies unfurl their tongues,
the bees thrum their eager wings,
the ferns wave their golden hands.

And you and I put on our golden shoes
and walk the golden-footed path,
kings and queens ourselves,
richly robed, this trembling.

WHEN THE LAKE IS CALM

When the lake is calm, no ship is real,
bow and stern as one, a cairn
suddenly built on the horizon.

Head on, a thousand feet of iron ore
lifts on the lake as on a ray of light.

Or as if a king, now a boy, who
will slowly grow to king again,
rides astride a barge of gold.

When the lake is calm, the tireless
bell buoy ceases to guard the reef,
bronze clappers so still we can lose our way.

Water world at peace, ships
tall as castles glide by, leaving a rise
and fall of kingdoms no one notices.

Paradise at hand, the king
floats like a happy child.
The sentinel bird atop the mast
today turns out to be a dove.

LATE SUMMER WIND AT DAWN
WELCOMES ROBERT BLY

Like stallions tethered to Roman chariots,
the muscular waves surge through the waist of the Straits.
Like legions they come.

The west wind has cleared up everything—
The stars! Far islands! Invisible springs!
Even an excitable double rainbow is only
dawn wearing a funny hat.

Yellow birds reappear from inside houses of cedar.
Serious crows patrol the golden ground.
Above us, waving arms of ecstatic gulls.

I have been awake and busy all night
so that this could happen. It was done
so that I could tell you—soon you
too will be wide awake and blazing!

(for a class and public reading on Mackinac Island,
August 18-19, 2010)

YOU KNOW YOU ARE AWAKE WHEN

You know you are awake when the ear
hears the difference between the groan
of cedar rubbing against cedar,
and the groan of a rope
straining a cedar limb.

When the bore of the wind,
the luff and spank of it, tipped
with ships horns, sounds
the sway of the sea itself.

When we elevate into ourselves,
into wind scrubbing the world clean,
a rough wind from the east, gray scuds
disturbing every bug, and we, no longer

anchored like ships in the lea
of the land above the twist of the sea
for succor, protected by the fog of sleep,

awakened now, as the bed
of the sea wakes, ruffles, curls,
cries, crests and tumbles
in gusts that topple the aged birch,
the too-tall cedar, several
worm-struck spruce and a grove
of blight-plagued beech,

the wind alive, the water alive,
the ships coasting at anchor alive,

and me and you alive, meeting dawn's expedient
interruptions of grandchildren settling grains into bowls
of trembling raisins, milk from Holsteins,

dry cedar for fire, lit with old dry news, a match,
then stories, the door of the human day blown
open, shining with the spat of flame,
singing with the clink of morning spoons.

POSTSCRIPT

SEEKING THE FULL AUGUST MOON

Good morning, class. The teacher you
expected, James Lenfestey, will be absent today.
He is in a kayak paddling toward the endless eastern
horizon of Lake Huron, already beyond the islands,
seeking the home of the full August moon.

Which rose last night in such ridiculous splendor
he spilled good wine all over himself
and salt caramel fudge sauce to boot
on his pale white shirt,
but the moon kept coming, and

although he knows the moon is not actually
as big as a dirigible, or as a Frenchman's hot air
balloon appearing from the pool of the lake
with a hidden fire raising it up in well-understood
inevitability, and yet

this pale orange now oblong and obstinate radiant being
arrived, on time, and again we were not expecting
its size and scope and winsome sadness.
Nor later its demanding brightness erasing all
but the most vigilant stars and constellations,

a monthly meteor moving at the pace of sleep,
there when you go to bed no matter how late,
there when you wake up no matter how early,
like 6 a.m. this August twenty-first, as the little
brown bats returned from their moonlit excursions

to their stately home behind the bedroom shutter,
crowded together after the excited liberty of gliding
back and forth like trout through silvery moonstreams,
now cozy as a dozen children snuggled in one bed

reading the wide-eyed astonishments of Hansel and Gretel,
Dr. Seuss, or The Night Before Christmas,
it makes no difference as all they will do, and soon enough,
is fall asleep in that upside-down way,
prattling on until their jaws slacken in sleep

about the size and shape and color of moonlight
tonight, the Sturgeon Moon the natives say,
but we bats, we really have no words for it, only
astonished cries, flight, sleep, and the desire
 to awaken again in its arms.

So we will have a substitute teacher
this morning, class,
the exhausted, bleary-eyed husk
hanging upside down before you.

ABOUT THE AUTHOR

James P. Lenfestey is a summer resident of the East Bluff of Mackinac Island, and has taught a poetry class at the Grand Hotel for the past 15 years. He is a former editorial writer for the StarTribune, where he won several Page One awards for excellence. Since 2000 he has published a collection of personal essays, six collections of poems, two poetry anthologies, and co-edited *Robert Bly in This World*. His memoir, *Seeking the Cave: A Pilgrimage to Cold Mountain*, was a finalist for the Minnesota Book Award, and his latest poetry collection, *A Marriage Book: 50 Years of Poems form a Marriage,* was a finalist for two Midwest Book Awards. As a journalist he has covered climate science since 1988. He lives in Minneapolis with his wife Susan Lenfestey. They have four children and eight grandchildren.